Discover Your Inner Startup

A Toolbox for Building an Innovative Company

Mel ARAT

New York City Books

Arat, Melih

Discover Your Inner Startup

Published by New York City Books

www.nycitybooks.com

Author's email: melarat@alumni.harvard.edu

Cataloging-in-Publication

1.Extraordinary 2. Creativity 3.Innovation 4.Self-Help

Discover Your Inner Startup

Mel ARAT

To the people who has courage to start a fire.

CONTENTS

Introduction

This book is aiming to help you discover your inner startup.

You know that deep in your heart you want to start a business, and you have some thoughts in your mind, but you are not sure which one is worth to pursue.

The second thing when you have a business idea, you need a plan to put it into practice. Without a well-crafted plan, a dream will remain a dream.

This book will help you to crystallize your business idea and create a roadmap for building your business.

In our daily lives, we are making observations, experiencing problems as a customer, and we have the insights into how we can improve an existing business service, or create a new one. So, we have it inside; but we don't know how to put it out. We don't know the ways to make it real.

Starting a business is about making hundreds of decisions. Usually, entrepreneurs know a few of the answers and try to answer the others along the way. This book is providing an opportunity to think deliberately in a logical sequence about every major decision without skipping anything substantial for business. This full-fletched guide includes entrepreneurial exercises that help you build your business brick-by-brick.

You will first take out your business idea, turn it into a future picture in your mind, and paint it through the pages of this book.

The book is designed by a step-by-step approach, and it is entirely different from a traditional business plan. A business plan starts with an executive summary, and it is the part that you write after you complete the business plan. Again in a business plan, you define the business in the beginning. However, in real life, there is a thought process about the problems of the customer and solutions for these problems. According to this book, a startup process begins with finding and making the business idea lucid. Then it continues with developing the value proposition. Later the entrepreneur starts to solve marketing, production, operation, and financial problems. Without a corporate philosophy and a people strategy, startup rarely last. Deciding on strategy is refreshing the mind, but founding a business requires more than this. You need to do financial projections and choose a legal organization type. This book is designed to be an efficient guide through all this stages.

In each chapter, the book gives place to some conceptual explanations and brief guidelines about the relevant stage of the business. After each concept, there is a template for creating ideas and making decisions. The reader becomes an entrepreneur and makes his/her choices using these templates throughout the book and builds his/her business.

The book's goal is to protect the entrepreneur from making mistakes, keep the costs low, and give exactly what the customers need while standing out in the market. The core idea is to create a successful business by minimizing waste of resources such as money, time, and human power in the startup stage.

Startup Founder vs. Entrepreneur
The two terms used interchangeably but they are not the same. An entrepreneur is an individual looking for business opportunities and profit. The entrepreneurs are interested in the business itself and profitability before its growth potential. A chef as an entrepreneur may be interested in opening his/her own restaurant and making it profitable as soon as possible.

On the other hand, a startup founder wants to build a growing business that will make an impact on the lives of people. He/she wants to find investors, create cool products, and generate larger profits in the future.

Of course, startup founders look for money; they want to convert the value of the company when they exit. The book primarily focuses on starting a business rather than selling it and that's why there is no chapter about the exit strategies. I wrote Discover Your Inner Startup to help people who want to build growing businesses. The book primarily focuses on starting a business rather than selling a business and that's why there is no chapter about exit strategies. The book has a systematic approach and both startup founders and entrepreneurs can use it.

"Don't worry about failure, you have to be right once."

Drew Houston,
Co-founder Dropbox

+

FINDING A BUSINESS IDEA

Finding a business idea

Some entrepreneurs have ideas in their minds, and they are very excited to go into business. Some other entrepreneurs have no idea to start their business. They only have an urge to start their business.
This chapter targets the second group and provides some templates to inspire business ideas.
As a reader, you are supposed to think and create some business ideas in this chapter. If you have an idea, this chapter still may offer a chance to reconsider your business thoughts in your mind.

Solve an existing problem

You can view any difficulty in life as a business opportunity. So, all of your problems might be a source of a business idea. Just scan your life and focus on the issues that you want to solve. Other people's questions or problems of the organizations might also be excellent sources of finding business opportunities.

Problem	*Example* Traditional Solution	The business Idea
My Problems Counting calories that I take	Writing them down	A smartphone app counting calories when you take the picture of the food.
Other People's Problem School success of a student	Hiring a private tutor and bearing some other costs such as transportation of the tutor	Online Private Tutoring
Organizational Problem Decreasing the cost of transportation of goods for a corporation	Buying trucks with low fuel consumption	A software that optimize the routes of the trucks

Solve an existing problem

Problem	Traditional Solution	The business Idea

Solve a future problem

The world is changing very fast.
Every day new technologies and new practices are being launched.
Every new technology comes with an opportunity.
When a new smartphone introduced into the market, a need for cases, chargers, and apps starts to occur.

Example

What are the new technology or practices of today?	What is the problem/opportunity that comes with it?	What might be the business idea that may occur with this new technology?
The electrical car	Charging the batteries in the rural areas	Selling a electrical battery charger unit to the gas stations in rural areas.

Solve a future problem

What are the new technologies or practices of today?	What is the problem/ opportunity that comes with it?	What might be the business idea that may occur with this new technology?

Create new solutions to the basic needs

Our basic needs are the same-the need for sleeping, sheltering, communication, or education. However, the solutions are evolving.

Airbnb provides a modern, homely and affordable solution while we travel. Still, we don't have a similar service for home food. We can think about a new solution for basic needs.

	Example	
Basic need	**Traditional solution**	**New solution**
Transportation	Private car or cab	UBER

Create new solutions to the basic needs

Basic need	Traditional solution	New solution

Help people save money

People usually like to do some savings. If you can find a solution to decrease the people's cost, your solution model may be a growing business.

Energy-saving or low-energy devices, collective or prior purchasing programs help people to save money.

Example

A product or service with regular price	A method or technology to decrease the cost	A product or service model idea based on saving
Music CDs	Downloadable Mp3 and streamlining	iTunes, Spotify, Pandora

Help people save money

A product or service already in the market with regular price	An alternative method or technology to decrease the cost	A product or service model idea based on the savings

Find a solution to make people's live easier

People tend to prefer simple solutions. Mechanical pencils took the place of the wood-encased carpentry pencils because it removed the need for a sharpener. Frozen foods made people's lives easier. There are still a lot of complicated things in life such as changing a flat tire or moving from one city to the another.

Example

Difficult and time consuming problems in life	A practical idea that can be a solution	A product or service model idea based on making people's live easier.
Selling unnecessary staff from home	Internet	Craigslist, Facebook market

Find a solution to make people's live easier

Difficult and time consuming problems in life	A practical idea that can be a solution	A product or service model idea based on making people's live easier

Make things and chores more entertaining

People are ready to spend money on entertainment. A robot shaped vacuum cleaner may look funny. A bicycle shaped pizza cutter may be decorative and entertaining.

	Example	
Boring tasks or chores in life	**A practical idea that can be a solution**	**An product or service model that comes with some sort of entertainment**
Brushing teeth	A music player attached to the toothbrush	Arm & Hammer Tooth Tunes Toothbrush "What Makes You Beautiful"

Make things and chores more entertaining

Boring tasks or chores in life	A practical idea that can be a solution	A product or service model that comes with some sort of entertainment

Make products smart

The new technologies give an opportunity to make everything smart. With an intelligent lock, you can remotely control your home door from your phone. A device that detects the increase of humidity level in your home can warn you about a potential leak, and you can take action before it is too late.

| | *Example* | |
Traditional stuff	**How can you make it smart**	**Product idea**
Mattress	Using a sensor and smart phone app	A bed that keeps track of your sleep.

Make products smart

Traditional stuff	How can you make it smart	Product idea

Combine different products

Combine two different products or their features and create a new product. Combination of an alarm-clock and espresso machine next to your bed is a great tool to awake. The sound of coffee-machine or the smell of the coffee can awaken you.

Example

Product/ Service A	Product/ Service B	Combination Product/ Service
stroller	bicycle	Combination of a stroller and a bicycle for mothers.

Combine different products

Product/ Service A	Product/ Service B	Combination Product/ Service

Turn your hobby into a business

There are many businesses created by the hobbyists.

Steve Jobs was a hobbyist of the electronics and built a computer business.

Terry Finley formed a company of racehorses. He bought a racehorse and started to sell partial ownership of racehorses.[1]

Focus on your hobby and see if you can start a business out of this hobby.

Example

Hobby	Business idea As products	Business idea as services
Chess Hobby	Producing and selling chess sets, books, souvenirs	Chess classes Chess clubs Tournament organizations

Turn your hobby into a business

Hobby	Business idea As products	Business idea as services

Sell an experience

You can start a business focusing on selling an experience. People are usually looking for a sophisticated experience after consuming all the stuff in their ordinary lives.

Working in a vineyard for a week can be an extraordinary experience for the wine enthusiasts, and they may like to pay more for it than for a vacation in an ordinary holiday resort.

Example

Target group	Business idea	Experience concept
Healthy-lifestyle people	Selling a farming experience	A day long experience in a real farm - Cow milking - Goat Milking - - Wool Bracelet - Making Brush a Sheep - Soak the Sow - Groom a horse - Collecting eggs

Sell an experience

Target group	Business idea	Experience concept

The Finalist Business Ideas

After thinking and elaborating many different ideas, you should pick one. To select a business idea, you may list your finalists, and you can score their likelihood of success.

Choosing a business idea is important because you are going to structure and for most of the business based on this business idea.

Don't try to find the perfect business concept because the products evolve and vary over the time. However, to start, you need to choose one idea.

Example

(Score ideas for each criteria. 1 is lowest and 5 is highest score)	IDEA Selling paper cups to coffee stores
The level of differentiation	1
Investment Cost	1
The size of demand	5
Competitiveness	1
Total Score	8

The Finalists

(Score ideas for each criteria. 1 is lowest and 5 is highest score)	IDEA 1	IDEA 2	IDEA 3
The level of differentiation			
Investment Cost			
The size of demand			
Competitiveness			
Total Score			
The Finalist Idea			

+

CUSTOMER PROBLEMS AND SOLUTIONS

Customer Problems and Solutions

In the first chapter, you try to find a business idea, and hopefully you choose one.

In this chapter, you focus on the business idea as a problem and solution. Customers are not looking for products. They are looking solutions for their problem.

You define a problem or a need in the market.

You go into detail and try to explain the difficulties that customers are experiencing and your solution for these instances.

You describe a problem and solution scenario that provides a basis for your company's product or service. Then, you summarize your solution regarding features and benefits.

The Aim/Need

The aim and need are different things. Define the aim and the need of the customer based on your finalist idea.

Example

Aim	Need
What is the aim of the customer in the field that you want to provide product or services? What is the thing that the customer is trying to achieve?	What is the need of the customer in the field that you want to provide product or services?
The customer aims to go to New York. He wants to see his family.	The customer needs transportation. The customer needs a technology to see his family.

The Aim/Need

Aim

What is the aim of the customer in the field that you want to provide product or services? What is the thing that the customer is trying to achieve?

Need

What is the need of the customer in the field that you want to provide product or services?

The Incident/ Problem

The incident and problem are two different things. Incident is an interruption of a service. The problem is the cause of this interruption. For example, the crash of software in a computer is an incident and the an error in coding is a problem. Incident is on the surface, and the problem is beneath it.

Example

Incident	Source
What is the incident that the customer is experiencing? What are the things that customer complaining about?	What is the source of the problem that causes the incident or complains?
The customer is complaining about the comfort of a sofa. It is hard as stone.	The root of the problem could be the design.

The Incident/ Problem

Incident	Source
What is the incident that the customer is experiencing? What are the things that customer complaining about?	What is the source of the problem that causes the incident or complains?

The Solution

What is your solution? In which way, the customer will feel satisfied? What is your solution scenario? Write a scenario example of a customer's problem and your solution for it.

Solution	Scenario
Interchangeable heels for woman shoes. Woman can easily change their heels for adapting occasion.	A woman starts her week day with her low heel (Number 1) shoes. She gets on the subway and stands comfortably. When she gets her office, she changes her heels and puts on high heels (Number 5). After a busy work day, before she leaves the office to meet her husband for dinner and she changes her heels with middle height heels (Number 3). When she gets home she peacefully sleeps without any pain in her feet. By using this new product she doesn't need to carry several pairs of shoes for different occasions.

Your Solution

What is your solution? In which way, the customer will feel satisfied? What is your solution scenario? Write a scenario example of a customer's problem and your solution for it.

Solution	Scenario

Your Solution Map

Illustrate your solution with graphics, pictures or flowcharts. You can also produce a video that explains your scenario.

Your Solution Map

The Features and Benefits of Product

Now, you describe the features and benefits of your product. Each feature should be described as a benefit.

Features	Benefits
Features are characteristics that your product or service does or has.	Benefits are the reasons customers buy the product or service.
For example, a battery may be 1800–2600 mAh. The feature usually doesn't mean anything for the customer.	A battery with a capacity of 1800–2600 mAh provides powerful, long-lasting energy for the customer. It means that your kid can play longer with his remote control toy car.

The Features and Benefits of Product

Features	Benefits

Barriers to Entry

Barriers to entry are obstacles that make it difficult to enter a given market.

Government Regulation
Is it hard to get government approvals for a specific business or product?

Start-Up Costs
What is the cost of starting a business in your field?

Technology
Is it a unique and protected technology by patents?

Economies of Scale
Does it require large quantities of production?

Product Differentiation
Is your product different than competing products?

Access to Suppliers and Distribution Channels
Could every firm easily buy or distribute their products in the market?

Barriers to Entry

Describe barriers to entry in the market for your product.

Describe barriers to entry created by your product and company for the competing products and services.

"Your customers are the judge, jury, and executioner of your value proposition. They will be merciless if you don't find fit!"

Alexander Osterwalder,
Value Proposition Design: How to Create Products and Services Customers Want

+

VALUE PROPOSITION AND BUSINESS MODEL

Value Proposition

Value proposition refers to a business or marketing statement that a company uses to summarize why a consumer should buy a product or use a service.

This statement convinces a potential consumer that one particular product or service will add more value or better solve a problem than other similar offerings will.

Example

UBER's Value Proposition

- One tap and a car comes directly to you
- Your driver knows exactly where to go
- Payment is completely cashless

What is your value proposition?

Crystalize your value proposition for the customer in a succinct and understandable way.

Business Model

A business model is a company's plan for how it will generate revenues and make a profit.

It explains what products or services the business plans to manufacture and market, and how it plans to do so, including what expenses it will incur.

There are many different types of business models. Direct sales, franchising, advertising-based and brick-and-mortar are all traditional business models. There is also a click-and-mortar business model, which combines a physical presence with an online presence.[2] Creating value comes with a cost. Any income incurs an expense. In your business model, you need to mention both incomes and major expenses.

You should define your sources of income in your business model. **Incomes**	You should have a sense of expenses. Without predicting the major costs, income projections will be useless. **Major Expenses**
• Sales of product and services • Rent income • Advertising • Royalties • Licensing fee • Interest income	• Rent • Salaries • Equipment • Material costs • Marketing and Advertising costs • Official licensing costs • Loan payments

What is your business model?

Where will your revenue and profit come from?	What will be your major expenses for your business?

"The basic approach of positioning is not to create something new and different, but to manipulate what's already up there in the mind, to retie the connections that already exist."

Al Reis,
Positioning:
The Battle for Your Mind:
How to be Seen and Heard in the
Overcrowded Marketplace

+

POSITIONING IN THE MARKET

The Market

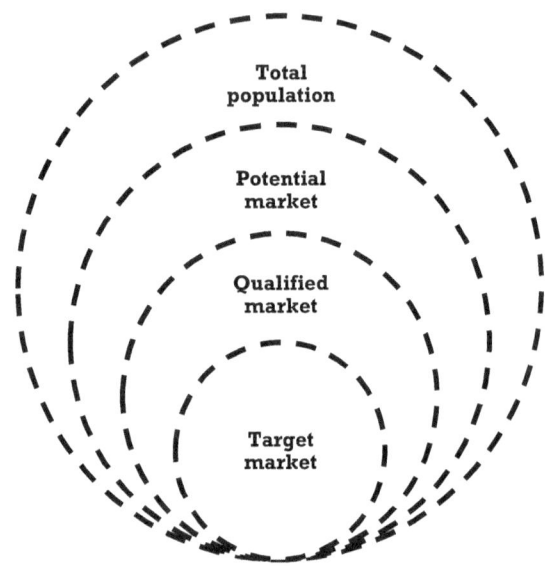

Total Population is all people in a particular market such as a city, state, country, or continent.

Potential Market is the people who have the interest to acquire the product or service.

Qualified Market is the people who have money and permit to buy the product. (e.g., Everybody needs transportation and may wish a luxury sports car. But this wish should be backed up by money and a valid driver's license.)

Target Market is a specific group of consumers at which a company aims to sell its products and services. A target market can be separated from the market as a whole by geography, buying power, demographics, and/or psychographics.

The Target Market

A market is the sum of all the buyers and sellers in the area or region under consideration. The area may be consist of a particular group of internet users, cities, regions, states, or countries.

In the first place, you have to consider the trends that shape your market. Is the market growing, stable, or shrinking? It is better to choose to invest in a growing market because a growing market will have more growth opportunities. In a stable and mature market, you need to be competitive to win some market share. You need to avoid to invest in a shrinking market since the market will disappear some time later.

However, a general market cannot be a target market. You have to focus on a specific part. The word "target" requires you to narrow down your focus. So, starting from the total population, you should decrease your market circle to your target market.

On the other hand, knowing the existence of a broader market will provide you a chance to evaluate different opportunities. In the future, you may like to change your target market within the market.

Market Trends

There are three types of trends that shape markets: Short-Term Trends, Intermediate-Term Trends, and Long-Term Trends. For a startup focusing on long-term trends will allow you to predict the future.

Trends that shape an industry are Technology Trends, Consumption Trends, Demographic Trends,
Political Trends, Legal Trends, Economic Trends, and Business Market Trends.

Each of these trends may have an impact on your market growth; it may increase or decrease the size of your market. Before you start a business, it is helpful to consider all these trends to make a conscious decision.

Example:
Market Trend Analysis of Electrical Car Business

Trend Area	Prediction	Impact on Business
Technology	Driverless Cars Longer battery Life	Better performance, More demand
Consumption	More eco-friendly customers	Growth in the market
Demographic	Millennials reaching the age 20-25	Selling more cars to Millennial generation
Legal	Legislations in favor of electrical cars	Decrease in the sales of fossil-fuel cars
Economic	More income per capita	More demand
Political	A positive climate supporting electrical cars	Lower barriers to the entry to the market
Business Market	More charging stations in the country	Electrical car becomes the new standard

What are the trends shaping your market?

Your Business:

Trend Area	Prediction	Impact on Business
Techno logy		
Consu mption		
Demog raphic		
Legal		
Econo mic		
Politica l		
Busine ss Market		

Market Segmentation

Market segmentation is the process of dividing a market of potential customers into groups, or segments based on different characteristics.
The segments created are composed of consumers who will respond similarly to marketing strategies and who share traits such as similar interests, needs, or locations.[3]

Bases of Segmentation
- Demographic
- Geographic
- Psychographic
- Behavioral
- Distribution

Target Market Demographics

Define your target market demographics.

Criteria	Target Market
Age	
Gender	
Income Level	
Education	
Occupation	
Marital Status	
Ethnicity	
Other	

Geographic Segmentation

Segment your customers geographically and calculate the potential size of the market

* **Market Size** = Number of customers x Average sales amount per customer

Country / State	Region / City	Number of customers	Average sales amount per customer	* Market Size

Behavioral Segmentation

Define your market based on your customer purchasing and consumption habits.

Criteria	Explanation
Usage rate of product (frequent, rare, etc.)	
Usage occasion (celebration, after meal, etc.)	
Usage size (a box, a bottle, can, etc.)	
The attributes of the product they want	

Psychographic Segmentation

Psychographic segmentation involves dividing your market into segments based on different personality traits, values, attitudes, interests, and lifestyles of consumers.

Example

What is the lifestyle of potential customers?	• Adventurists • Traditional Families • Urban couples
What are their values?	• Volunteering • Innovation • Eco-friendliness • Simplicity • Health • Putting education to No:1 priority
What are their interests and activities?	• Work • Outdoor sports • Concerts • Hobbies • Vacation
What are their attitudes?	• Frequent fliers • Buying in bulks • Investing on crypto-currencies

Psychographic Segmentation

Using the table below, do psychographic segmentation of your potential customers.

What is the lifestyle of potential customers?	
What are their values?	
What are their interests and activities?	
What are their attitudes?	

Distribution Segmentation

You can reach your customers in various markets through different channels of distribution such as supermarkets, department stores, wholesalers, or online platforms.

Example

Where do your customers buy your products?	Channel Name	% of Customers
Channel 1	Online Platforms, Amazon.com	%20
Channel 2	Department Stores	30%
Channel 3	Hypermarkets	20%
Channel 4	Company Stores	30%

Distribution Segmentation

Where do your customers buy your products?	Channel Name	% of Customers
Channel 1		
Channel 2		
Channel 3		
Channel 4		
Channel 5		

Positioning

The position is the place that the brand first conquers and then occupies in the minds of customers, relative to competitors products. When one customer identifies a particular brand with a specific word, this word becomes the position of the brand. One of the most successful examples of positioning is Volvo. Wholefoods identifies itself with organic and healthy food. Volvo positions itself with safety. A customer who is sensitive to safe driving buys a Volvo car because in this customer's mind safety is equal to Volvo. Wholefood is the first choice that comes to mind when one thinks about organic food.

Microsoft in its foundation years was successfully identified itself with the operating system, and later office programs. So, anybody needed an operating system or word processing and worksheets remembered Microsoft.

When you earn your place in the consumers' mind, sales becomes automatic. Branding and brand positioning is a long journey, and when a company determines its positioning, in the beginning, it may have more chance to be a leader in the minds of potential customers.

Examples

Brand	Positioning
Mercedes	Luxury
Chipotle	Quality Mexican Fast Food
Dollar Shave Club	Low Cost Humorous Shaving
Gillette	The World's Best Shaving
Apple	The Company that changes the world

Positioning Strategy

Create your positioning strategy by using the 5 steps template.[4]

Define the Target Segment Focus only on the main group of customers	
Find Differentiation Point Describe why you are different from your competitors	
Provide the Proof List the reasons that support your positioning claim	
Craft the Positioning Statement Write one sentence to explain the value that you are offering	
Create Positioning Slogan Make it simple, short, and catchy	

Final Market& Segmentation Decisions

After all of these exercises, it is time to finalize your decisions about market and segmentation.

What is your market definition?	What specific segment of the market you want sell your services and products?

Final Customer& Positioning Decisions

What are your final decisions about customer and your positioning?

Who is your ideal customer?	What is your preferred positioning strategy?

"If You're Not Embarrassed By The First Version Of Your Product, Probably you spent too much time on it."

Reid Hoffman
Founder, Linkedin

+

MINIMUM VIABLE PRODUCT (MVP)

MVP-Minimum Viable Product

Minimum Viable Product (MVP) is a prototype with minimum features to receive feedback from potential customers. The feedback process provides a sign to go or no-go for a more substantial investment.

Usually, startups go straight forward to product development and manufacturing process without getting the market approval. And if markets reject the product, then all the investment is wasted.

It is better to test a product idea with MVP concept in the early stage rather than getting rejected by the market.

MVP Example

A visual example may make it easy to understand. Imagine that you came up with the idea of a glass cup for the first time in the world. Before launching the production process, you make a paper cup and ask the opinion of potential customers about this cup. Based on the data you collect, you continue your design work.

Paper Cup   **Glass Cup**
MVP   **Product**

Before you design a glass, craft a paper cup, and ask the opinion of potential customers, how much they want to spend on this cup.

The Minimum Viable Product-MVP term was coined and defined by Frank Robinson[5] about 2001 and popularized by Eric Ries.[6]

Benefits in MVP

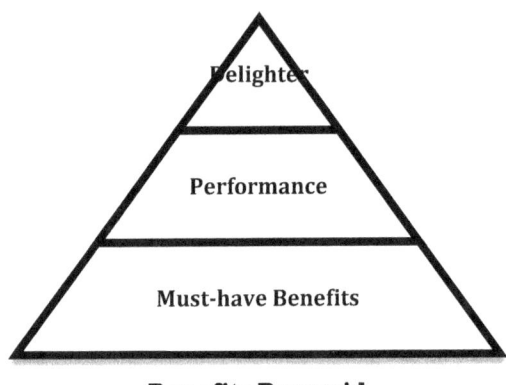

Benefits Pyramid

There are three types of benefits in MVP concept.

Must-have benefits
These are the benefits relying on the essential features of the product. Most likely all competing product provide these features.

Performance benefits
These are benefits that are competitive and satisfactory for the customer.

Delighter benefits
Delighter benefits exceed the expectations.

Defining your MVP Benefits and Features

Customer's perspective	**What are the benefits your customer is expecting?**	Entrepreneur's Perspective	**What are the benefits of your MVP?**
Is it delightful?		Features exceeding expectations.	
How is the performance and usability?		Feature design.	
Does it meet my needs?		Must-have features.	

Testing your product concept by MVP

A startup can use Minimum Viable Product concept for marketing purposes as well as product design.

For example, a startup can examine the performance of its marketing material, websites, and level of financial support from the market and investors.

Regarding products, there are also tests that a startup can receive qualitative and quantitative feedback.

Testing your product concept by MVP

	Qualitative Tests	*Quantitative Tests*
Marketing Tests	Marketing materials	Landing page Explainer video Ad campaigns A/B tests Crowdfunding
Product Tests	Hand Sketch Wireframes Mockups Prototypes	Fake door Product analytics

Marketing Material Tests

Marketing materials are a landing page, a video, an advertisement, an email, a brochure and so forth.

A landing page is a standalone web page, created specifically for a marketing or advertising campaign. It's where a visitor "lands" when they have clicked on a Google AdWords ad or similar.

A startup can produce a video and place it on the landing page and different platforms. The number of viewers, their comments could be useful feedback.

Advertisements on the web are quite measurable, and they are useful to get feedback about the ad itself and the product concept.

Product ads and brochures by emails are also helpful to see the effectiveness of the designs.

Above mentioned tests are an attempt to understand how compelling customers find this marketing material and why.

Marketing Material Tests

What are your marketing materials that you want to test?

Landing page	
Product Video	
Ads (for web and for printed media)	
PDF Brochure	
Other	

Quantitative Marketing Tests

Landing page
In landing page, you describe the product to potential customers, and if they are interested in, they sign up and leave their contact information.

Explainer video
An explainer video introduces the product, and then interested people sign up for additional information.

Ad campaign
Ad campaigns are necessary to drive traffic to your landing page or explainer video.

A/B Testing
In A/B testing, you create two alternative designs and compare the how they perform in the eyes of potential clients. Both of them could be alternative landing pages, and you can find out the one has a better sign up rate.

Crowdfunding
Crowdfunding platforms, Kickstarter or Indiegogo can be a great way to test whether or not people are willing to pay for your product.

Quantitative Marketing Tests

What are your plans for running below marketing tests?

Landing page	
Explainer video	
Ad campaigns	
A/B tests	
Crowdfunding	

Qualitative Product MVP Tests

Hand Sketches
Before mass producing the product, it is better to test the product with a hand sketch. A sketch on paper sometimes can be very useful to get potential customer feedback.

Wireframes
Wireframes are a step ahead of sketches. They are three-dimensional visual designs without details such as colors, images, and, fonts. They are the structure or the skeleton of a product.

Mockups
Mockups look much more like final product; they convey visual details.

Prototypes
Prototypes are closest to the actual product.

Qualitative Product MVP Tests

What are your plans to run the below MVP Tests?

Hand Sketches	
Wireframes	
Mockups	
Prototypes	
Other	

Quantitative Product MVP Tests

Fake Door Test
The fake door test is an effective way to learn the demand for a new feature you have in your mind. You include a button for this feature on your page and count the number of clicks. The button doesn't have functionality but shows the interests of the people.

Product Analytics
Product analytics help to get insights about customers and how they are using the product. By this test, you can see which features they use most and where they spend most of their time.

Product A/B testing
In product A/B testing, you can observe the performance of the user experiences of two alternative designs of one product.

Quantitative Product MVP Tests

What are your plans to run the below MVP Tests?

Fake Door Test	
Product Analytics	
Product A/B testing	

"Strength doesn't come from what you can do. It comes from overcoming the things you once thought you couldn't."

Rikki Rogers

+

COMPETITION&
SWOT ANALYSIS

Competition

Competitive analysis is very important for startups. A founder of a startup may think that his business idea is brand new and there is no competition in the market and this is not true. There is always competition.

First, when you find a brilliant idea, usually there are minimum five other people on the earth who came up with the same concept or a similar one. So, don't think that you are alone. The winner will be the best marketer and best practitioner in the market. In other words, the one who creates a buzzword about his startup and who quickly puts his ideas into practice will win the competition.

Second, you may think that your product meets an unmet need or meets the requirement better than the others. If there is a need, it means that people are meeting this need with a certain way. It may be a substitute product, a combination of products, custom or in-house solution. All of these products and solutions are your competitors. You have to examine these competitors and develop strategies to cope with them.

Main Competitors

List your competitors and the strengths and weaknesses of each.

Competitors	Strength	Weaknesses

Direct Competition

List and describe the competing product or service .

Direct Competitor	Product	Features and Benefits	Price

Indirect Competition

List and describe the indirect competing product or service.

Indirect Competitor	Product	Features and Benefits	Price

SWOT
Analysis

Strengths describe what an organization excels at and separates it from the competition.

Weaknesses are areas where the business needs to improve to remain competitive.

Opportunities refer to favorable external factors that an organization can use to give it a competitive advantage.

Threats refer to external factors that have the potential to harm an organization.

SWOT Analysis of Your Business

Strengths

Weaknesses

Opportunities

Threats

"Marketing is no longer about the stuff that you make, but about the stories you tell."

Seth Godin,
All Marketers Tell Stories

+ MARKETING PLAN

Marketing Mix

The Marketing Mix, also known as the 4 Ps of Marketing, is the combination of product, price, place (distribution), and promotion. When you make your decisions in these four fields, you can think that your marketing strategy is pretty much ready.

4Ps of marketing provides a sturdy base for a clear marketing strategy. 4Ps of marketing are like the four legs of a chair. They need to be in harmony. Your price strategy should comply with your product strategy, and your place (distribution) approach should match your promotion strategy.

The method was first created in 1960 by E. J. McCarthy.

Marketing Mix

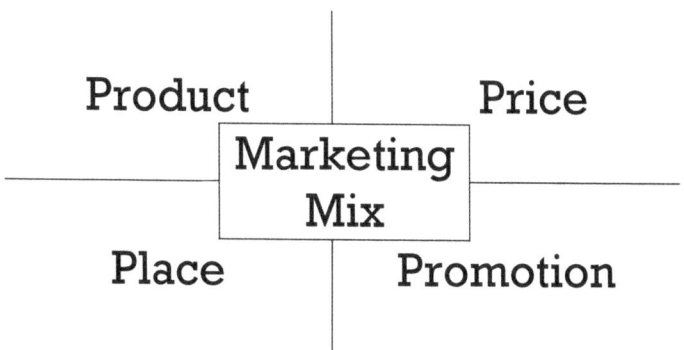

Product
The goods and services designed for customers.

Price
The strategic pricing of the product to keep the image of the product and company.

Place (or distribution)
The delivery or distribution process of products and services.

Promotion
The advertising, marketing, and sales activities that try to increase the sales of the product an services.

Product Strategy

A company is more than a product. A company is like a mother that gives birth to children. Apple company is not the MacBook Air, iPod, or iPhone. The products are temporary. When times change, products change. On the other hand, The entrepreneur builds the business around a product. If the product is successful like iPhone, then the company is successful. That's why the product strategy is the most crucial component of the marketing mix. As an entrepreneur, if you have the right product, you are on the right track.

You have to answer specific questions to develop a product strategy.

- How do you define your product? What are the primary attributes and benefits of the product?
- What will be the quality level?
- Will it be open for customization?
- Will there be a design difference?
- What will be the name of it?
- What will be sizes of this new product?
- Will there be an added value in packaging?
- Will you stand out regarding your warranty or return policy?

Your answers should be strategic and thoughtful because this makes the difference in the market.

Your Product Strategy

Criteria	Your Strategy
Product definition	
Quality level	
Customization Level	
Design Attributes	
Brand , product, model name	
Sizes	
Packaging	
Additional Services	
Scope of warranty	
Return Policy	

Place and Distribution Strategy

Place and distribution strategy is an essential part of the marketing mix. A smart distribution plan can determine the success of a business. Wal-Mart's decision to move the hypermarkets from city centers to the outside of the city was crucial to its success. Locating the stores outside of the town, decreased the cost of the property and provided more space for the store and parking.

In the 1980s, Apple and Dell companies sold their computers directly from the factory by getting orders on the phone. By not using traditional distribution channels such as wholesalers and not paying commissions, they increased their profits.

A well-designed distribution strategy can help to the market success. Distribution should not be just a task or operation in the business; it should be a strategy. So think about it deliberately, check what the successful companies are doing regarding logistics and benchmark them.

Your Place and Distribution Strategy

Criteria	Your Strategy
Transport, Warehouse management	
Distribution to Wholesaler, retail stores	
Distribution to our retail store/s	
Distribution by mail	
Franchising	
Inventory levels	
Vehicles to be used in distribution and transportation	
Alternative distribution channels	
Unconventional distribution channels.	

Promotion Strategy

Promotion Strategy usually defines the success of startups. You may have an outstanding product, but if nobody knows about it, you cannot sell it. At the beginning of its entrepreneurial journey, Apple made an immense entrance to the market with its "1984" advertisement.[7] This unforgettable bold commercial opened the doors of global success to the Apple. The Body Shop's founder Anita Roddick in its growth years decided to do Public Relations rather than advertising, and this strategy helped the company to save money to spend on social and environmental projects.[8] A strategic approach to promotion makes a big difference in a startup's lifecycle.

The promotion strategy consists of the sales organization, public relations, advertising, and sales promotion.

Sales organization is about your sales force. You may use your people to make the sales, or you can use distributors sales force to sell your products.

Public Relations is trying to take place in the news by creating social responsibility campaigns and other events.

Advertising is creating advertisements for television, printed media, billboards, or social media.

Sales promotion is using media for a limited time to increase the sales and consumer demand. Sales promotion includes contests, coupons, freebies, product samples, and so on.

Your Promotion Strategy

Activity	Your Strategy
Advertising Media: Billboards, Radio and TV	
Advertising Media: Magazines and Newspapers	
Advertising Media: Google and other social media	
Message Frequency	
Sales Force: Number of Sales People and Teams	
Public Relations Strategy and Campaigns	
Direct Marketing	
Social Media Marketing Strategies	
Other promotional campaigns	

Pricing Strategy

Pricing Strategy is one of the vital components of the marketing mix. It determines the fate of the startup. The customers make their final purchasing decision by price. If the customers don't think the product is worth it, they will not buy it. Tesla company decided to address the high-end market in the beginning, and their car prices were very high. This high price strategy helped the company to position the cars as state of the art. Beside company needed money to invest in the factory and high margins helped to sustain the new investments. Dollar Shave Club entered the market with the promise of a cheap but quality shaving experience. The low price entry strategy maintained company a huge success.[9]

Pricing strategy could be a key to enter a market. Usually, a high-price is the sign of quality, and low price is the sign of a wish to address large number of people.

When you set your price, you also define your target market. Discounts, coupons, and rebates, and sales campaigns are also practical tools to drive the demand.

Your Pricing Strategy

Price strategy	Your Strategy
Competition Based Pricing	
Customer Segment Pricing	
Market skimming pricing	
Market penetration pricing	
Allowances – e.g. rebates for distributors	
Payment terms – credit, payment methods	
Discounts – for customers	
List Prices	

"Leaders win through logistics. Vision, sure. Strategy, yes. But when you go to war, you need to have both toilet paper and bullets at the right place at the right time. In other words, you must win through superior logistics."

Tom Peters

+

SUPPLY MANAGEMENT STRATEGY

Sourcing

The sources of your products determine the quality of products and service. Usually, the stability of a supplier guarantees the success of a business. Think about McDonald's. The quality of meat, buns, and potato are defining factors of McDonald's business success. Starbucks also heavily rely on its suppliers. Can you imagine what happens when paper cup leaks or coffee machine serves warm coffee?

There are for critical dimensions of supply management.

- **Price.** The price is essential because your costs define your profitability.
- **Order Fulfillment.** The capacity, ease, and speed on order fulfillment are critical. The vendor should be able to supply large quantity of the goods when you need them. The ordering process should be easy. You should be able to place an online order. When you give your order, the supplier should be ready to ship the goods in a short period. If the supplier ships products in 30 days, it means that you should always have stocks for 30 days.
- **Quality.** The consistency of the quality influences your business. The fluctuation in the quality of the products has an impact on customer satisfaction. You lose customers if there is an inconsistency in your products and services.
- **Payment terms.** The payment terms are also mattering is supply process. The advance payment requirements or payment within 60 days after the placement of order have an impact on your financials.

Supplier Evaluation

Supplier
Scores (1 is the lowest and 10 is the highest)

Vendors	A	B	C	D
Criteria				
Quality				
Ease of order				
Capacity				
Speed				
Payment				
Price				
Total				

Technology

The technology, the machines, and methods that you use in your operation define the performance of your business.

Technology increases the efficiency of operations. A robot can make a car at half of the time 50 person. In warehouses, robots decrease the time in shelving and costs. In office operations, computer programs usually create unbelievable efficiency. Self-service technologies are taking the place of call-centers. Websites, social media, and smartphone apps change the business landscape.

A startup should decide the technologies it will use in two dimensions. First primary technologies that enable the company to do its business; and supplemental technologies to do its day-to-day operations.

Technology Choices

What are the critical and supplemental technologies that you will use in your business?

The name of the machine	Brief description	Cost Estimate

Strategic Alliances& Partnerships

Strategic alliances, such as co-marketing, co-production, co-development, and cooperative arrangements may help the growth of businesses. Linking your promotions, supply, or distribution strategies to another company or companies could improve the performance of your operations.

A strategic alliance is an agreement usually between two parties to reach a common business goal. The logical reason to form an alliance is to use the other party's strengths and resources. When both companies benefit from this alliance, they continue to this partnership.

The alliance could be in supply relationship. While one company (A) sells the product, the other one (B) produces the product. The market success of company "A," will create a positive effect on the sales of company B.

Collaboration Field	*Example* Partners	Collaboration Activity
Logistics	P&G and Wal-Mart	P&G and Wal-Mart use electronic data interchange technology and improves inventory efficiency of baby diapers.

Strategic Alliances& Partnerships

Which companies could be a good fit for an alliance in your business field?

Collaboration Field	Partner	Collaboration Activity

Good leaders have vision and inspire others to help them turn vision into reality. Great leaders create more leaders, not followers. Great leaders have vision, share vision, and inspire others to create their own. "

Roy T. Bennett,
The Light in the Heart

+

Vision, Mission, and Strategic Plan

Vision

A vision statement reflects where you want your company to be in the future. "Future" is usually defined as long term. A vision describes the "what" you will succeed in the future.

A vision should be bold and inspirational.

A strong vision comes with a simple of measure of success and call to action.

Amazon's vision statement is "To be the Earth's most customer-centric company, where customers can find and discover anything they might want to buy online."[10] Amazon's vision statement is simple and clear. They will do anything to be the most customer-centric company, and regarding action, they will provide everything for the customers on the online platform.

Your Vision Statement

What will you succeed in the future?	What is simplest indicator that shows that you perform towards yours vision?
What is the primary action that you will take towards your vision?	What is your vision statement?

Mission Statement

If vision where you go, the mission is how you go there.

Mission describes what, why and how you do. A mission statement could broaden your choices, and narrow them. Harley-Davidson mission statement is "We fulfill dreams through the experience of motorcycling, by providing motorcyclists and the general public with an expanding line of motorcycles and branded products and services in selected market segments."[11] According to this mission statement, they are narrowing down their field; it is motorcycle business and not automobile business. With this mission statement, they also broaden their field of activity, they also sell the Harley-Davidson branded products. Moreover, they explain why they are in this business. They want to fulfill dreams of their customers through the experience of motorcycling,

Your Mission Statement

What will you do to achieve your vision?	What will you avoid to do to achieve your vision?
How will you do it?	**What is your mission statement?**

Action Plan

Any business can only be successful through a dynamic action plan. You need to set goals and priorities to reach your vision.

An action plan improves the efficiency of using your time; it helps you focus on the essential task on time.

Useful goals clearly state what you want to accomplish, when you want to achieve it, how you're going to do it, and who's going to be responsible. Each goal should be specific and measurable.

An action plan may be regarding human resources, marketing, operations, supply management, financial management, and so on.

All plans may not go through, but at least they guide and push the entrepreneur towards the vision. Plans those are put into practice show which strategies work and which don't. The best plans are not the rigid ones; they are the dynamic ones which can change and adapt.

Example

Task or Project	Measurable Goal	Deadline and responsible person
Website	Completion of a full-fledged ecommerce site, entry of 450 products to the site.	1/1/20..

Your Action Plan

1st Quarter of your business

Task or Project	Measurable Goal	Deadline and responsible person

Your Action Plan

2nd t Quarter of your business

Task or Project	Measurable Goal	Deadline and responsible person

Your Action Plan

3rd Quarter of your business

Task or Project	Measurable Goal	Deadline and responsible person

Milestones

Milestones are installed to provide reference points along the road. In Roman Empire, the milestones were used to reassure travelers that the proper path is being followed, indicating either distance traveled or the remaining distance to a destination.

In business, milestones are specific targets used to mark particular points along a timeline. These points are the signs that indicate a phase is completed and a new phase is ahead, they may signal anchors such as a start and end date, a need for external review or input and budget checks, among others.

Your Business Milestones

Milestone	Business Field / Department	The Target Completion Date

"A highly developed values system is like a compass. It serves as a guide to point you in the right direction when you are lost."

Idowu Koyenikan,
Wealth for All: Living a Life of Success at the Edge of Your Ability

+

CORPORATE PHILOSOPHY AND VALUES

Corporate Philosophy

Most of the entrepreneurs start their business with a product idea in their mind. When they find the necessary resources, they launch their business. However, the companies with just a product in their portfolio, when they confront an obstacle on their journey, they don't know how to respond to their obstruction. Entrepreneurs need guiding principles to stay in their tracks. The entrepreneurs who started today's largest corporations, they had a corporate philosophy in the very beginning.

Wholefoods core values form their corporate philosophy, and by these values, they know what they will do when they come to a crossroads.

Wholefoods Core Values[12]

- We Sell the Highest Quality Natural and Organic Foods
- We Satisfy and Delight Our Customers
- We Promote Team Member Growth and Happiness
- We Practice Win-Win Partnerships with Our Suppliers
- We are part of an interdependent business ecosystem.
- We Create Profits and Prosperity
- We Care About our Community and the Environment

A useful corporate philosophy helps a company develop a particular corporate culture, and employees.[13] It also positions the values of the company in the minds of others both within and outside of the organization. Your corporate philosophy should give employees a starting point for the decision-making process, so they are all operating on the same page.

Your Corporate Philosophy and Values

Domain	
Customers	
Products and Services	
Innovation	
People (Stakeholders)	
Suppliers	
Environment	
Profit	
Leadership and Management	

Your Corporate Philosophy

A corporate philosophy does not always fit in a template. So, use these two blank pages to write down your corporate philosophy.

Your Corporate Philosophy

"Design is the silent ambassador of your brand."

Paul Rand

+

CREATING AN IDENTITY

Creating a Name

Principles for Creating a Company Name

A good company name may provide an advantage for a startup. Think about Alibaba.com. A Chinese company became the world's number one eCommerce platform. Its name helped the company to grow internationally. The guideline below can help you to consider name alternatives.[14]

- Avoid hard-to-spell names. (Food2Go)
- Assess if the name is catchy. (BestBuy)
- Don't pick a name that could be limiting as your business grows. (Brown Computers)
- Use a name that has meaning to it and conveys a benefit. (Whole Foods)
- Don't use a generic name that doesn't mean anything. (Books)
- Make sure you can trademark the name. (America)
- Choose a name that appeals not only to you but also to the kind of customers you are trying to attract. (American Girl, doll company; Dollar Tree, convenience store)
- Don't pick a name that is long or confusing. (Boston Market, it is a chicken restaurant)
- Get the ".com" domain name.
- Be creative. Combine something that is already familiar to your potential customers and something unique to your company or product. (Apple, it is the Apple, once that made Adam and Eve, rule breaker)
- Reflect your business philosophy. (BestBuy)
- Geographical names such as America, Europe, or New York create an impression of a larger company. (American Life)

Creating Your Company Name

Company Name Alternatives	Finalists	Final Decision

Logo Design Principles

The logo may be a key to success for a startup. Think about the logo of Coca Cola. This unique logo created a distinctive perception for the company.
Use below principles as a guideline.[15]

- Understand your business brand and reflect it in your logo.
- Customers should find your logo unique and easy to perceive.
- Keep the design simple. The best logos evolved towards their purest form in time.
- Use colors strategically; associate the right color with your business philosophy and positioning.
- Make it scalable and versatile. Make it versatile enough to look equally stunning on business card design, letterheads, banner ads, brochures or business websites can go a long way in making it a timeless artwork.
- It should look great in black and white.
- Make it a memorable and timeless design.
- The logo should be appropriate for its intended audience.
- If it is a memo product, you can use an animal with a sharp memory such as an elephant (e.g. Evernote).

Logo Design Workshop

Pick an animal or object that symbolize your business or company.	Choose colors relevant to your business.
Define the universal symbols that represent the benefits of your products and services.	Find out the possible distinctive visual aspects of your business.

"In fact, leaders of companies that go from good to great start not with "where" but with "who." They start by getting the right people on the bus, the wrong people off the bus, and the right people in the right seats. And they stick with that discipline—first the people, then the direction—no matter how dire the circumstances."

Jim Collins,
Good to Great

+ PEOPLE STRATEGY

Advisory Board

An advisory board is a small group of advisors for the startup. Knowledge is the highest leverage that one startup can use. Usually, founders of startups could be experts in the field of the product but may insufficient in the functional areas of business such as accounting, marketing, social media, human resources, and finance. They can use the expertise, advice, and network of the members of the advisory board. Learning the tips and tricks of a particular field may take years, but your advisor may know and share them with you.

Advisory board members can be active professional managers of corporations such as accounting or finance manager of a firm. Retired people or temporarily unemployed people with necessary skills could be good fits for advisory boards.

You can define the number and fields of advisory members by the nature of the business. The board members of a service and production company can be a lot different.

You can start for looking advisory board members from the people you know. Former colleagues and acquainted people may be part your advisory team.

Advisory Board

List the members of the advisory board. Include their brief backgrounds and organizational roles.

Domain	Name	Expertise and Experience
Accounting and Taxes		
Finance		
Management		
Marketing		
Human Resources		
Law		
Technology		
Social Media		
Media Relations		

Creating a People Strategy

One of the defining factors in a startup is the people strategy. Apple became a successful company because, from the very start, they tried to hire the best people available in the world. McDonald's founder Ray Kroc, designed a business that the ordinary people can perform. Starbucks is coffee shop chain, but it is a company more about people. All the employees are supported to have a health insurance and higher education. So, usually, the entrepreneurs believe that their success is based on a brilliant product. But they need to keep in mind that anything in the company is the work of employees. They run the business. Your employees will determine you will be a startup or start down.

You should think about your people strategy. When we use the word strategy, it should be something different than the ordinary. It should be unique; it should contain intelligence.

Regarding people strategy, you should develop plans for hiring, rewarding, compensation, training, promotion, and creating a culture.

Creating Your People Strategy

Domain	Strategy
Hiring	
Rewarding	
Compensation	
Learning, Training and Development	
Retention	
Promotion	
Developing Culture	

Management Team

The management team is responsible for running the company.

Chief Executive Officer-CEO is the primary person who layouts the corporate strategy, does critical networking for business, hire the first and critical people, and solves the major problems of the startup.

Chief Operations Officer-COO is the person who builds and runs the day-to-day operations of the company such as production, purchasing, shipments, and so on. Before Chief Human Resources Officer is assigned, COO hires the people for operations.

Chief Technology Officer-CTO is the one who crafts the technology in the company. Most of the startups are in the field of technology and while CEO solves business problem CTO is responsible for choosing and developing the technology for the firm.

Chief Marketing Officer-CMO prepares the marketing plan and puts it into practice. Creating the corporate identity, deciding for the advertising and social media strategies, solving problems of packaging and so on are some of the responsibilities of CMO.

Chief Finance Officer-CFO manages the finances, plans for the future. CFO creates budget and financing strategies. Especially in startups, CFO is the person that keeps the company on track and prevents it to go into bankruptcy. Because the money is like the air for the company if it goes below the minimum levels company dies, no matter what.

Your Management Team

Position and Name	Responsibility	Required Competence
CEO		
COO		
CTO		
CMO		
CFO		

Organizational Structure

An organizational structure defines the lines of authority, hierarchy, and accountability. The organizational chart shows the pattern or arrangement of jobs and groups of jobs within an organization.

For a startup, it is useful to have a bird's eye view of the company. You can efficiently use branches and sub-branches to develop specialized departments and positions.

Example

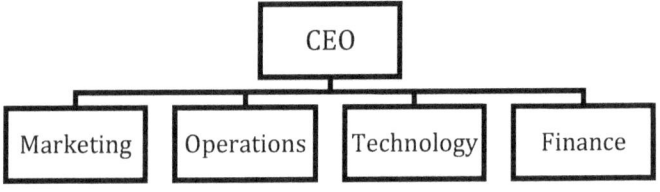

Organizational Structure

Draw your organizational chart below.

Staff Plan

Staff plan is needed to hire the people to run the company. First, you need to decide the organizational structure of the company, and then the people that will work in these departments. You should define each position with an aim, a set of tasks, and required skills for this position.

Staff plan helps to predict the cost of operations. You can budget not only the salaries, but the necessary office space, furniture, computers, and all other relevant costs.

Your Staff Plan

Department	Job Title/ Qualifications	Annual Salary / Cost	Assigned Personnel

> *"If you
> cannot explain
> it simply,
> you don't understand well
> enough."*

Albert Einstein

+

CREATING A PITCH FOR YOUR COMPANY AND PRODUCT

Creating a Pitch

A pitch is merely delivering a business plan verbally. An entrepreneur pitches his business idea to the prospective business investors or partners. An elevator pitch is simply a concise presentation that explains the idea less than a period of an elevator ride. A video pitch is a pitch done via a short video rather than in person. The aim of the pitch is introducing a business opportunity with the intention of acquiring funding for the company.[16]

In your pitch, you should describe your company and product briefly. In a scenario setting, you should present the problem and your solution. Your difference and competitive advantage should be clear. Regarding money, tell what the investors will gain if they invest in the business and ask the amount that you need for your company.

The Pitch

The Questions	Your Answers
What is the business?	
What is the product or service?	
What is the problem of customer?	
What is the solution?	
What will the investor gain from the investment?	
What is the amount of investment that you ask from the investors?	

*"If you can look into the
seeds of time,
and say which grain
will grow and
which will not,
speak, then, to me."*

**William Sheakespeare,
Macbeth**

+

FINANCIAL PROJECTIONS

Funding Your Startup

You need to fund your business idea. How can you get your business off the ground?[17]

Using your own money

You use your own money, savings, and earnings to fund the business. You can sell your property. If the company goes bankrupt, you lose your own money.

Friends and Family

Borrowing money from friends and family could be the first option to start a business. They may be more willing to help you to found your company. It may be easier to convince them, on the other hand, it may harm your relationship if you can't pay their money back on time.

Trade Equity or Services

You can trade some of your skills to get some services. A chef needing a professional kitchen can offer a company to cook lunch for them and ask for free use of the kitchen in the evenings for your business.

Small Business Loans

Some banks offer loans to small businesses, but banks will make it sure that you have collateral. It can be difficult to qualify.

Small Business Grants

Non-profit organizations and government organizations offer grants to small businesses. These grants might be small but very useful for starting the fire.

Accelerator

Business accelerators and incubators have sprung up all across the world,

Accelerators are organizations that offer a range of support services and funding opportunities for startups. They provide mentorship, office space and supply chain resources. More importantly, business accelerator programs present opportunities for accessing to capital and investment in return for startup equity.

Contests

Business idea and plan contests could be challenging, but if you win, you will have a certain amount of funding. Even if you lose it, it is an excellent chance to purify and promote your business idea. They are also a great way to practice your pitch for the other investors.

Crowdfunding

If you have a marketable idea and you're great at creating an attractive video crowdfunding might be an option. Crowdfunding platforms Kickstarter and Indiegogo bring people and entrepreneurs together.

Sales Forecast

Sales forecasting is the process of estimating future sales. For predicting sales, you can use several numbers, but if you use an inductive approach, your projection can be more realistic. In other words, if you try to calculate your potential sales, try to figure out the number of sales visits in a day, week, month and year. Then multiply the number of customers and the sum of your average sale. Let's imagine; you have a coffee shop. Each customer leaves USD 10 average. You expect 100 customers in a day. So, USD 1000 is your average sales. Your annual sales should be around 350 thousand dollars.

Sales forecast usually accompanies cost-of-sales. It helps to calculate gross profit. You should subtract your costs from your sales revenue, and you can find your gross profit. The costs can be salaries, rent, supplies, utility bills, and so on.

Year 1 Sales	Months													
Product	1	2	3	4	5	6	7	8	9	10	11	12	Annual Sales	Annual Profit
a														
b														
Total Sales														
Cost of Sales														
.... expense														
.... expense														
Total Sales														
Gross Profit														

Year 2 Sales	Months												Annual Sales	Annual Profit
Product	1	2	3	4	5	6	7	8	9	10	11	12		
a														
b														
Total Sales														
Cost of Sales														
.... expense														
.... expense														
Total Sales														
Gross Profit														

Year 3 Sales	Months											
Product	1	2	3	4	5	6	7	8	9	10	11	12
a												
b												
Total Sales												
Cost of Sales												
.... expense												
.... expense												
Total Sales												
Gross Profit												
Annual Sales												
Annual Profit												

Startup Investment Requirements

Startup Expenses

Startup expenses occur before the beginning of the business. For example, many new businesses incur expenses for legal work, logo design, brochures, site selection and improvements, and other costs.

Startup Expenses	
Legal	
Stationery etc.	
Brochures, Business Cards	
Website and Internet services	
Consultants	
Insurance	
Rent and Deposits	
Research and development	
Furnishing and Renovation	
Other	
Total Start-up Expenses	

Startup Investment Requirements

Startup Assets

Startup assets are a little different from expenses. An asset is cash or anything of value that can be converted into cash. Typical startup assets are cash, equipment, office furniture, computers, machinery, and so on.

Startup Assets	
Startup Inventory	
Cash requirements	
Office equipment (Computer, printer, etc.)	
Furniture	
Production equipment	
Expensed equipment (revenue generating expenses)	
Other	
Total Start-up Assets	

Total Investment Requirements	
Startup Expenses	
Startup Assets	
Total Investment Requirements	

Break-Even Analysis

Break-Even Analysis is used to predict the point when the company starts to make a profit. The company begins the entrepreneurial journey with always fixed and variable costs, at one point sales revenue equals total cost and this point is called Break-Even point. At Break-even point, there is no profit or loss. The firm merely covers its total costs. After reaching Break-Even, the company is making money. The Break-Even analysis is essential because by using this method, an entrepreneur can make a realistic prediction of his net income. Before that, all the money inflow goes the costs.

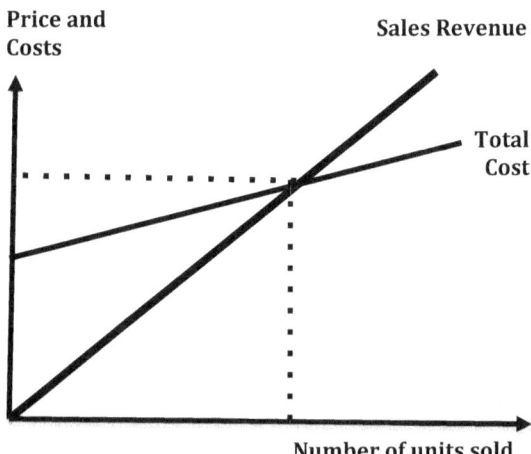

Break-Even Analysis Graphic
Revenues (Sales Income) = Total Costs
at Break-even point

Total Cost, Variable Cost, and Fixed Cost

Variable costs are costs that change with changes in production levels or sales. Variable costs in a restaurant are the food costs. When they have more customers, they serve more food and the cost rises.

Fixed costs remain roughly the same regardless of sales/output levels. Examples include: Rent, Insurance, and Wages.

Total Cost merely is Fixed Costs and Variable Costs added together.

Total Cost = Fixed Cost + Variable Cost

Total Costs include some of the Variable Costs then Total Costs will also change with any changes in output/sales.

If output/sales rise then so will Total Costs.

If output/sales fall then so will Total Costs.

Sales Revenue is the number of products sold multiplied by the price of the product.

Sales Revenue=Sold Units x Sales Price

Break-Even Analysis Example

ABC Book Store
Fixed Costs:

Rent	: USD 4000
Sales Assistant (Wages)	: USD 2000
Total Fixed Cost	**: USD 6000**

Variable Costs:	**Selling Price:**
Books: USD 10 per book	Books: USD 20 per book

So we know that:

Total Fixed Costs	= USD 6000
Variable Cost per Unit	= USD 10
Selling Price per Unit	= USD 20

We must firstly calculate how much income from each bunch of flowers can go towards covering the Fixed Costs. This is called the Unit Contribution.

Selling Price –	Variable Costs	= Unit Contribution (Profit)
USD 20 –	10	= USD 10

For every book sold USD 10 can go towards covering Fixed Costs. Now, let's calculate how many units must be sold to cover Total Costs (FC + VC). It is called the Break Even Point

Break Even Point (Number of units)=	**Fixed Costs /**	**Unit Contribution (Profit)**
600 Books =	USD 6000 /	10

Your Break-Even Analysis

You can calculate your Break-Even Point by calculating your Unit Contribution and Fixed Cost. Fill in the table take the sums. Then divide the fixed cost by unit contribution number; this will give you the number of units to reach Break-Even Point.

Assumptions:	
Average Unit Sale	
Average Per-Unit Cost	
Unit Contribution (Profit)	

Calculating Fixed Cost	
Rent	
Utilities	
Insurance	
Salaries, benefits, etc.	
Other Total	
Total Fixed Cost	

Break Even Point (Number of units)=	Fixed Cost /	Unit Contribution (Profit)

Projected Profit and Loss

The Profit and Loss Statement also is also known as Income Statement. This statement helps us to understand if the company is in lose or making a profit.

It starts with Sales Revenue then it shows Direct Costs (or COGS, Cost of Goods Sold). When we subtract Direct Costs from Sales Revenue, we get the number of the Gross Margin. In other words. Sales less Direct Costs gives us the Gross Margin.

The cost of goods is different from operating expenses. We buy a product from a factory, and we pay 2 dollars for each product and sell it for 3 dollars. So, our direct cost is 2 dollars. Operating expenses are any expense which is not part of the cost of goods sold such as rent, insurance premium, salaries, and so on.

From the gross margin, we subtract operating expenses and we reach the gross profit.

Gross Profit is also called EBITDA for "earnings before interest, taxes, depreciation, and amortization."

| Sales | – | Cost of goods | = | Gross Margin |
| Gross Margin | – | Operation Expenses | = | Gross Profit |

Months

Year 1	1	2	3	4	5	6	7	8	9	10	11	12
Sales Revenue												
Cost of Goods												
Gross Margin												
Less Op. Exp												
Salaries												
Rent&Utilities												
Advertising												
Sub Total												
Gross Profit												

Cash Flow Statement

Cash Flow Statement is a financial statement that summarizes the amount of cash and cash equivalents entering and leaving a company. Cash Flow Statement helps us to understand how a company's operations are running, where its money is coming from, and how money is being spent. It also helps to project the periods when the cash outflow is larger than cash inflow. If the incoming amount of money is less then the outgoing amount, the business owner can take a loan to make the payments. Cash Flow Statement is crucial since it helps investors determine whether a company is on a solid financial footing.[18]

Cash Flow Statement doesn't provide information about profit or loss; it only shows the financial health of the company. The company could be making a lot of profit, but if it cannot manage its cash flow, it cannot make the payments of salaries, loans, or vendors.

If your cash flow statement is frequently giving a negative balance, you have to find more investment to fix your flow.

Before you create a cash flow projection for your business, it's important to identify your key assumptions. Key assumptions should relate to two primary areas:

Receivables: These assumptions should outline how quickly you receive payment from your customers. For example, if most of your customers pay you within 30 days, a key assumption could be: 90% of sales will be collected the month after the sale.

Payables: These assumptions should outline when your payments are due. For example, if your vendors require payment within two weeks of delivery, a key assumption could be: Payables are due within 14 days of purchase.[19]

Projected Cash Flow

	Month 1	Month 2	Month 3
Beginning Cash Balance			
Sources of Cash			
Receivable Collections			
Customer Deposits			
Loans from the bank			
Other			
Total Sources of Cash			
Uses of Cash			
Payroll and its taxes			
Accounts Payable-Vendors			
Other overhead-Including Rent			
Line of Credit Payments			
Long-Term Principal Payments			
Purchases of Fixed Assets			
Estimated Income Taxes			
Other			
Total Uses of Cash			
Total Sources of Cash			
Total Uses of Cash			
Balance			

Balance Sheet

The balance sheet is a snapshot at a single point in time of the company's accounts – covering its assets, liabilities and shareholders' equity.

The purpose of the balance sheet is to give users an idea of the company's financial position along with displaying what the company owns and owes.

The layout of a balance sheet reflects the basic accounting equation:

Assets = Liabilities + Owners' Equity

Assets are the things your practice owns that have monetary value. Your assets include items such as cash, inventory and property, and equipment owned, as well as marketable securities (investments), prepaid expenses and money owed to you (accounts receivable) from payers. Assets also include intangibles of value, like patents or trademarks held.

Liabilities reflect all the money your practice owes to others. This includes amounts owed on loans, accounts payable, wages, taxes and other debts.[20]

Owner's equity represents the owner's investment in the business minus the owner's draws.[21]

Your Balance Sheet, Year 1

Assets		Capital and Liabilities	
Cash		**Liabilities**	
Bank balance		Accounts Payable	
Accounts Receivable		Short-term debt	
Inventory		**Total Liabilities**	
		Capital	
		Paid-in Capital	
		Earnings	
Total		**Total**	

Your Balance Sheet, Year 2

Assets		Capital and Liabilities	
Cash		**Liabilities**	
Bank balance		Accounts Payable	
Accounts Receivable		Short-term debt	
Inventory		**Total Liabilities**	
		Capital	
		Paid-in Capital	
		Earnings	
Total		**Total**	

Your Balance Sheet, Year 3

Assets		Capital and Liabilities	
Cash		**Liabilities**	
Bank balance		Accounts Payable	
Accounts Receivable		Short-term debt	
Inventory		**Total Liabilities**	
		Capital	
		Paid-in Capital	
		Earnings	
Total		**Total**	

+

LEGAL ORGANIZATION FORM

Legal Organization Form

There are five common organizational types (also called "legal structures") for small businesses.
- Sole Proprietorship
- Partnership (general, limited, & LLP)
- Limited Liability Company (LLC)
- C-corporation
- S-corporation

Factors for Choosing an Organizational Type

Taxation – *Taxes on profits are paid through personal tax returns except for corporations.*
The level of taxes changes from one organization type to another.

Liability and Risk – *Responsibility for harm to another person or property, or contract disputes.*
Some organizational types limit the personal liability and some not.

Management – Decision-making authority.
Some of the organization types provide full authority in decision making and in some types you need to share the authority.

Continuity and Transferability – *How a business persists and how it is sold.*
Some corporations are created by shares and it is easier to sell them partially.

Expense and Formality – *Costs, legal responsibility, the degree of complexity.*
Founding some organization types is cheaper and easier regarding formalities.

Sole Proprietorship & General Partnership

Sole Proprietorship
Business is one and the same as the owner.

Advantages and Disadvantages
- Owner has unlimited personal liability.
- The taxes are reported on the owner's personal tax return.
- Owner controls business.
- It is the simplest form of organization.
- It is the lowest cost to form.
- It is appropriate for small start-up.

General Partnership
A general partnership is an association between two or more people in business seeking a profit. Like a sole proprietorship, partnerships have pass-through taxation and owners are personally liable for the debts of the business. General partnerships can be created with little formality, but because more than one person is involved, a written contract stipulating the terms of the partnership, called a "partnership agreement," should be created.

Limited Liability Company (LLC)

A limited liability company (LLC) is a corporate structure whereby the members of the company cannot be held personally liable for the company's debts or liabilities. Limited liability companies are essentially hybrid entities that combine the characteristics of a corporation and a partnership or sole proprietorship. While the limited liability feature is similar to that of a corporation, the availability of flow-through taxation to the members of an LLC is a feature of partnerships.

Although LLCs have some attractive features, they also have a number of disadvantages, especially in relation to the structure of a corporation. An LLC has to be dissolved upon the death or bankruptcy of a member, unlike a corporation, which can exist in perpetuity. Also, an LLC may not be a suitable option when the objective of the founder is to eventually become a publicly listed company.

The primary reason an LLC is selected as an ownership structure is to limit the principals' personal liability. An LLC is often thought of as a blend of a partnership, which is a simple business formation of two or more owners under an agreement, and a corporation which is afforded certain liability protections.

C and S Corporations

C-Corporation

The C-corporation, also known as a "regular corporation," is the most common form of business entity for larger companies. Unlike sole proprietorships and partnerships, corporations are separate and distinct from their owners in the eyes of the law. As a separate entity, corporations have several distinguishing characteristics including limited liability, easy transferability of shares (this is, ownership), and perpetual existence. Corporations also have a centralized management which may be different persons from the owners.

Advantages and Disadvantages
- Limited liability
- Company is taxed (double taxation an issue)
- Complex to form
- Complex ownership and management
- Appropriate for a few specific reasons – otherwise, choose another organizational type

S-Corporation

Owner has limited liability of a corporate shareholder but pays income tax like a sole proprietor or partner.

Advantages and Disadvantages

Same as C-corporation except for pass-through taxation.

An S-corporation is a regular corporation that has elected "S-corporation" tax status. Forming an S-corporation lets you enjoy the limited liability of a corporate shareholder but you pay income taxes as if you were a sole proprietor or a partner.

What will be your organizational form and why?

A lot of entrepreneurs prefer to found a company in the form of a Sole Proprietorship or an LLC. Since, the word startup has a potential for growth, an LLC might be a better choice.

You know the pros and cons of each form What is your final decision?

"Do you want to know who you are? Don't ask. Act! Action will delineate and define you."

Thomas Jefferson

Your Next Move:

Ready,
Aim,
Found!

Sources

[1] Terry Finley, How I Made My Millions: Are You Willing to Go All In?,
https://www.cnbc.com/id/44205150

[2] What is a 'Business Model.
https://www.investopedia.com/terms/b/business model.asp.

[3] Track Maven, Market Segmentation.
https://trackmaven.com/marketing-dictionary/market-segmentation/

[4] Donatas Jonikas, 5 Steps to Create Effective Positioning For Your Startup.
https://slovakstartup.com/2017/08/01/5-steps-positioning-startup/

[5] Frank Robinson, A Proven Methodology to Maximize Return on Risk, 2001,
http://www.syncdev.com/minimum-viable-product/.

[6] Eric Ries, The Lean Startup, Currency, 2011.

[7] Steve Johnson, What you didn't know about Apple's '1984' Super Bowl ad,
http://www.chicagotribune.com/entertainment/tv/ct-apple-1984-ad-myths-ent-0205-20170201-column.html

[8] James Bethell, Body Shop changes strategy on public relations,
https://www.independent.co.uk/news/business/body-shop-changes-strategy-on-public-relations-1442891.htmlapp

[9] Leonie Roderick, Dollar Shave Club's secret to

marketing success: 'Bite down on a human truth and don't let go',
https://www.marketingweek.com/2017/06/26/doll ar-shave-club-unilever/
[10] Amazon.com's Vision Statement
http://panmore.com/amazon-com-inc-vision-statement-mission-statement-analysis
[11] Dan McCarthy, Mission Statement
https://www.thebalancecareers.com/strategic-plan-elements-2276139
[12]WholeFoods Core Values,
https://www.wholefoodsmarket.com/mission-values/core-values
[13] Sampson Quain, Examples of Corporate Philosophy,
http://smallbusiness.chron.com/examples-corporate-philosophy-37868.html
[14] Company Name Principles
Yanik Silver. 7 Tips for Naming Your Business.
https://www.entrepreneur.com/article/223401
Entrepreneur Staff. How to Name a Business.
https://www.entrepreneur.com/article/21774.
Richard Harroch.12 Tips For Naming Your Startup Business.
https://www.forbes.com/sites/allbusiness/2016/10 /23/12-tips-for-naming-your-startup-business/#4c673ead904e.
[15] Roy Miller. 6 Basic Principles Of Logo Design.
https://www.designhill.com/design-blog/basic-principles-logo-design/.

Henry Kel. Top 7 Logo Design Tips To Create A Timeless And Creative Logo. https://www.designhill.com/design-blog/logo-design-tips-create-timeless-logo/.

Jacob Cass. Vital Tips For Effective Logo Design.https://www.smashingmagazine.com/2009/08/vital-tips-for-effective-logo-design/

[16] Alan Gleeson,The Business Pitch, http://articles.bplans.co.uk/starting-a-business/the-business-pitch/407

[17] 9 Realistic Way to fund your startup, https://www.startupgrind.com/blog/9-realistic-ways-to-fund-your-startup/,

The 10 Most Reliable Ways to Fund a Startup, https://www.entrepreneur.com/slideshow/299773

[18] What is Cash Flow Statement, https://www.investopedia.com/investing/what-is-a-cash-flow-statement/#ixzz5Ip0HxKBu

[19] Creating a Cash Flow Projection, https://wellsfargoworks.com/management/article/creating-a-cash-flow-projection

[20] Financial Statements 101: How to Read and Use Your Balance Sheet, http://www.apapracticecentral.org/business/finances/balance-sheet.aspx

[21] What is owner's equity, https://www.accountingcoach.com/blog/what-is-owners-equity